DAY
BED

Daybed

Zach Savich

Black Ocean
Boston · Detroit · Chicago

Black Ocean
P.O. Box 52030
Boston, MA 02205

blackocean.org

Cover & Book Design by Nikkita Cohoon | nikkita.co

ISBN 978-1-939568-23-6

Names: Savich, Zach, author.

Title: Daybed / Zach Savich.

Description: Boston : Black Ocean, [2017]

Identifiers: LCCN 2017047854 | ISBN 9781939568236 (pbk. : alk. paper)

Classification: LCC PS3619.A858 A6 2017 | DDC 811/.6~dc23

LC record available at https://lccn.loc.gov/2017047854

FIRST EDITION

For Hilary, and Loughran

Contents

But does a Human Form Display
To those who Dwell in Realms of day

—Blake

I. *West Durham Street*

Like seeing a movie in the day in another city

Foundling dove
I rest my hammock on the grass

Grew able to read only when very aroused
Could we be reading the same line now

Or say this is heaven
And there is no heaven

So only this remains

They have another dish for the fallen petals

Flowers cut from larger petals
Some features' fineness is comparable to beauty

The prettiest words refer to passing time
Is mercy an exception or the only one

Can delicacy be enough
If insistent enough to endure

Is it delicacy then

If you are thirsty it is too late

But if there may be gradations of thirst
There was this sweet bolt new bark grew around

And new shapes to lock bikes to
Could it matter what the confetti is made of

Asparagus by the road
A child made a radio by resting anything in a creek

An acrobat didn't love me

Presently blackbirds

I watch some hammer a patio into the air
Anything a blackbird does is clean

I turn in the substantiating breeze
Purity arises variegated, nuanced, involved

Did not the wilderness of precision
Double the switchgrass

Seeing you tripled the pear

Civilization forgets its raincoat in the cab

I hoped to be older when driven to Proust
The melody being whatever you repeat

Beautiful warbled hopscotch grid
So you see a person in a car for sale in a field

The past wasn't simpler but memory is
My neighborhood has its own stained glass shop

I offer the business I can

Bees made the calendar

Totally honey
Graceful in the sufficient gauge

So pluck out a world and carry it before you on a dish
I'm in this jacket I wear through every season

If I took it off it'd be trash
I'm wearing this stupid hat so you won't

Remember me pretty

One taught me to ascend a steep hill

Bend double and swing your arms foolish
I left the shower so we could see

A divot in the glass confirmed
If air is involved in the workings of a mirror

All air must similarly convey
As oranges preserved in straw and heat

Every accent trills

Trees in this week before there's any thought of blossoming

When bare wood in sun
Is more than enough

Take-out guy idles by the longest vent in this city
I tighten by hand the reachable bolts

I have a face that shows what I've seen
One touched my tongue and said it should feel like this when
    you say it

I'm as happy as an easel in a bin of onions

The kind of chair you can stack or leave out

Even inferior fruits are improved by ripening
Like someone too old to rake—but it's all right, it's summer

They fill whatever you have with paint
They fill whatever you have with wine

At a pace that has steadily never in history occurred
These tomatoes are wildly improved by being eaten

I'll go when the wind stops

The melody being whatever you repeat

The window closes only enough
One cleanses by abrasion, by peonies

By the first flying bird set down
And flight was just another thing there was

By dedicate the song when it's done
I say the first flying bird was a honeyeater

I say spring is our first evening together and if there are no
  others all right

II. Prose

I arrive in wind and a street fair
Wind chimes 40% off

40% of a wind chime is the sound

One tires of the beyond

*

Now bend or extend the hurt part

Odysseus ties himself to the mast and wails
Fish are ripples, which research accounts for
Children are windowsills
Some statues require willows

Bird's eye view: a term for meeting a sparrow's gaze

*

I wanted to bring you berries but also to appear with nothing
   but my white shirt

I take the earliest bus and pretend to read
Flood slow enough, who can say how much is lost to steam

Years later the emperor returned the borrowed bicycle

Time healed me of prose

*

Duration is good

I stand in my white shirt with my jacket gone
If I should live so long
With my white shirt gone
To stand with the buttons in my hand
Bouquets just from brushing through

*

The tone is bereft
Steam rose into a good museum and the first horses
The first movement moves past, careless for return
Children rolling hills, tossing dust from a field
Say as far as the world goes, it's Saturday
Is someone telling the story
Of causes

Here's a church so pretty, you shouldn't mind just walking by

III. Mt. Airy

When I was born death was walking

A horse into a field
Letting it go

Should it have rained and who are you in this
And will the horse my friend survive couldn't matter

Better to watch a vase on a bed
Sure, but what must I become

To ask my friend this horse to return

If the dead have preferences they must prefer the future tense

Will you be sitting by a window in this year
As though asking affirms

What wouldn't they affirm
Shirt hung for a curtain

Having washed it in the sink each night
My ship will be the turning one

Its sail is shining rain

Important to also imagine paradise

Harbor where the wind begins
In the shadows in the vines

Love is redundant, indefensible, effortless to disprove
Fragility was of value or was a value

When I was alive somebody ordered an extra coffee
Beside me in arboresque rain

Here you are

Wondrous to pad the end of a ladder

Or lumber too long for a truck
With knotted wreath or traffic cone or duct-taped oven mitt

Wondrous to massage hail from a paw
Wondrous the tuning, continual and arch

Or new places for launching a canoe
An appropriate guest, in this life

I dry my hands on the towel's back

Folly to mourn

Sparrows in the nick of time
Or a window's dress

I do
I do mourns completely

Once Jay found a hundred dollars
Bought three hundred in oysters

Sparrows do alternate takes enough to count us through

Consciousness doesn't recommend itself

Sufficient labor
Find radishes

Somebody dumped this traffic cone in the woods
Stained past signaling, I depend on it

I carry the railing there, a pile of cut-up shirts
What'd they get into, was a man there

Have I seen his dog

I wouldn't finish a race if I could see the end

I don't have to
They load a thing in rain

I put my chair where I can see my better chair
Hand where the wine is, lightest fizz in it

Would you call it fizz
There is an early train, or early enough

I give my ticket to someone who disappears down the street

There was this plow you led around by being there

Take your shoes off to cross the creek, leave them
Coffee is a little kid

Forever wants another thing
Give it what it wants, what choice is there

It's not broken it just stays outside
Its being broken is just about its staying outside

It has done well at staying outside, so is broken

Early apples lighter than the lightest leaves

Bricks the shade of a horse in other grass
In wind more real than really real, in grasses known for quail

Which direction is the siren coming from
Which direction is the fire

Thick rugs draped on a fence
They beat the shrubs like rugs to get the petals out

Petals in the shrubs like dust in a rug

I see one gardening, alive nearby

Total extinction will be a moment now
I'm asking for a friend

I've never done anything for a day
Teeth, I won't need you

Still, eternity can't get over us
What's an apple blossom to you

No one here but your bracelet on my watch

IV. Free Books

I'll take the free books when they're a little rainier
Only dawn and already the street singer's voice too delicate to hear
Berries so bright the morning should look dark beside them
Should we place the flowers behind or in front of the curtains?
Behind
So you will have to open the curtains to see the flowers and
There's a good day

*

I saw the subway singer drop his instrument and wail
It was soft and very appropriate
Somebody lashed the guitar to his throat so it wouldn't be hurt
    if he kept dropping it
I wanted a breeze to cool him so much, I thought he produced one
I wanted a prayer like *Let every season be the season*
Do not breezes more easily the grasses play than this harp it is
    calluses to master
Tear one, play it, throw it in a stream
Evening is a deck of cards

*

In the wood block print the simple dark of the bear's hide is
achieved by thirty whumps of the press. The dark of the mouth by
twenty. Or the idea that the amount of sense is directly related to
the passions of the speaker. If sense means sensation, and so. Or

how many minutes would most stand the balloon artist failing to produce even an unrepeatable shape. *I'm leaking* cries the stroller thing and mom tongues the cone. These monologues tragic for being monologues in a play. Tuned by the abandoned song, past windows without glass, so anything you see passes through.

*

Or one running the instrument in
In snow

Has been running since before snow

Softer, after marigolds aren't

*

The ripest braid and bear fruit underground
Faithful to fertility that does not only reproduce

Before the kettle sounds, it quiets minutely
The safest place to conceal a diary is in another's house,
    another's handwriting
I shower before phoning
If you won't tell me what's at the top of the trees, I'll dig
Water these at night

*

In her last tale cobblers were required to hold unclaimed boots
    twelve years
It has been twelve years
The abundance of unclaimed boots in the square, in her last tale
Eyeglasses and hay represent foolhardiness
A pitcher by the bed means it is a guest room
A pencil in the vase means there is yarrow in the vase
The dog is learning to walk again
First one foot, then any foot

V. Friends of the Wissahickon

Spraypainting the bicycle

I had higher hopes for the shape it would leave on the fence
Every panel is a gate

Anywhere you put the vase will be eye level
This vase packed in marigolds and steam

Meanwhile, leaves that fall so far should have two names
By now the tulips are grown enough for school

I'll walk them

Three years married, I understood fidelity

There's nothing to it
Like daylilies staying alive so easily you shouldn't call it that

There you are
Brushing your teeth in the parking lot

What's the other difference
I assumed every poem indicted the sun

Just how I saw it

I carried the stairs

Hollyhocks, centaurs
Grief thinned me so I appear irredeemably young

Then my hangovers just stopped
What do bees know

There's more honey in my mouth
One touches tenderly the conjurer's hands

How do they remain

Days like searing the sun in butter

I miss the earliest train, am here another month
Little white fish in a pail

Ribbons in your hair faded to a color
There's enough electricity in the human hand to operate a piano

I used to fly to beaches in spring, what I thought were beaches
Was spring

My shirt open to the bottom of my shirt

Our letters were like inventing the steam engine

So one morning in a derelict station
Someone could open a café

To sidle is a motion bringing one closer regardless
Letters like strawberries on a plain cloth

I stay on the smaller balcony
Pull the curtain around the gardenia

There's a lemon under that bowl

Easy magic: put a free sign on anything

Poof, there it goes, careworn, susceptible, anew
Will the river change or the rocks

Or: what isn't already free (disappearing)
This is where you go in, holding a glass above the water

It is a thing you are doing so I can watch
I bend to the glass

I save especially the husks

Or the worn part of a wood chair

Put more paint there next time
Or the same amount but thicker

One's voice ages not even saying anything
Birds go into the shed and don't come out

Like one too old to rake, pocketing each leaf
The way I stand at this window

You'd think the sun goes down

Flour I brushed from my shirt months ago

Under the snowmelt, on the patio bricks
I wake early and forget everything

I pass a taxi driver singing or loudly listening
Loudly listening? I'll take it

Two giraffes and a duck, impervious helium, in the trees
There is no specific tool for removing them

Somebody starts to ascend and is told that's no one's job

I wouldn't write a novel for my life

I taste the rock to confirm
A "found dog" poster

One method is leave the dough alone for months
More heat from the yeast, and months, than from kneading

Funny to have forgotten which way is upriver
I narrow my eyes, just to see

Like one too old to rake, sweeping leaves toward a drain

Bicycle in vines

Child singing with mouth against the window
A way of seeing out

Shh somebody says, so she begins to whisper-sing
How does it change the view

Blue comb in her hair, orange comb in her hand
Pockets for anything sewn on the gold skirt

She and I'll be at the river

VI. Instead of Reading

For this to survive suggests devoted worlds
How many days has it been
Count our letters

*

Different blue of a field up a hill from a sea
The mind hurts, though
Because so much it knows has already happened
Much as dressing well in the clothes one has, in any year
Or how, in love, a season rarely finishes in a season
But is it not also a garden
To take an interest in
Moss on a stone or
A stone

*

To take, for example, the air

As the tide revealed interiors, yet it was better when the
    water returned
Preceded by gulls and steam
Or white dragonflies in green mud, ridged wings
Half-built places in a landscape assuring currency better than
    a bank
So much invested in the elements

Flowers visible just in the peripherals
Can you gather them astride
O gather them if you don't look!

Devotion ardors
Always toward the soft yes
Coincidenced by the full chord
Dragonfly at a bottle rim
We have emptied it for it
Fittingness in the burnished stems

Instead of reading

VII. Already

Dogs on a roof

Among laundry and vines
My ears just popped

I can still feel the hospital bed whenever I want
It is sometimes very light, a cape or caterwaul

Dogs on a flat concrete roof
While the earliest buds hunch the tree double

It's like turning on a light exactly as bright as the room

Metal bits on the metal table

They rust immaculately
I decide to be more assailable, like a paper boat

Children slide boards into the chainlink gaps
Half-boards, actually, reeds

Some spend all day patching the sun, brandishing scarves
Better to note the copper flashing on the smallest birdhouse

Or this wire somebody wound around my thumb

The laundry gets brighter the longer it's out

Somebody wants me to care about arguments
Care is an argument

I could fix this window or live here a while
One sauce is only parmesan and egg

Implicit heat is enough
There are miles outside

I've never seen a crow

The coffee stays warmest longest when I drink it

Lying on the daybed, with vases
Like one too old to rake, waiting for wind

Winnowing is worth more than wit
The forest burns itself whenever it wants

It's not dramatic, birds crashing up from the ashes
Ordinary finches

Their population doubles whenever they want

Divination outlasts the divine

One morning my mother swept the butterfly bush
Stirring what draws them

I'm happy enough watering soil
Or rubbing lilac on a drumhead to tune

Though every singer has already died
And every painting is of paradise

You know because you can hear them

One lives twice, but how to tell if this is the latest aspect of
    the first

Fruit trees dying from unimpeachable effulgence
Lashed to the house or each other

You have to follow this thing to see if it's a compass
Pretense is exactly half

The trail neglected enough
I walk on a fallen tree

Dog in his first days of feeling tired

I wash everything with only my hands

I love my wife because 4 PM is not 3 PM
Her bicycle asleep in my car

The light now is trustworthy and very new
Too hot to hold

Hold it with two hands
You shouldn't name a dog after anyone you've known

But name it

Gateways without gates, just a trellis, the stone path

I find whatever I take is a vitamin
Window planters holding nothing, they are for lease

Can it be the last one the indefinitely lasting one
Park in the middle of whatever this is

Meadow is a duration, barrow is
Yet to never be the voice expounding

I turned the corner of this page a year ago, I smooth it

In the photograph I will seem to be walking

Painted pinecones on the walk
Cathedral pigeons

Do you gather the pinecones in a pile and paint them and
    scatter them
Or paint them carefully where they are

What year is it again
Autumn was a cardboard box of crab shells and leaves

I find all the books are not enough

Bouquet swept through the basin of a fountain

Replenishes it, winnowingly
I'd say the trash sack on the window mends enough

They put the same things out to sell each year
All is only a dollar

So labor turns to care, like the singer who lost the contest,
    clarifying
I just wanted to put each note where you could really see

Soccer ball never reaching the river

VIII. A Smear of Paint to Test the Paper

1

I've already written.
    Now a chess set from petals, stems.
This bead is the bishop.
It moves like this.

    Why would the finale be any longer?
Dogs have to eat.
    Snow in the theater:
paper, soap. Foam
softly on the fool's brow.

2

Now the parade of dune blossoms.
    They seem taller,
when the sand goes.
    Love, the rainy season lasts.
Boats, stay home.

Have you been in jacaranda time,
    and endured?
        You've looked at the waterfall
long enough, and birds
singing a suckling song.
They avoid the windows, stream
    to each other.

3

  There's time for the bus
or a sandwich. Anywhere you see
  is moving faster, calmly now.

Cowslip is some kind of bird.
  If thoughts are starlings in a garden,
passing, on a branch,
    wire, now beyond sight, near rivers
elsewhere, catkins, wind-pollinated,
passing for time.

4

Oh, the day was already unbearable.
How often should heart tonic be used?
I supposed possibly usually,
    all being exculpatory enough.

    Time resumes in a fern. It isn't sad.
Soldiers remove the eyes
of a tethered goat. The mind is dry moss
        on white rocks.
Everything alive is original.

5

Hand me the last page.
Shine on the picture frame—
    the point of the picture.
        Pollen's best idea
    on a tarp on my car.

Dawn is another. Mountains begin
        in meadow naps, each clement span.
Lightning revives in a rowboat.
The final look looks up.
    What dwelling shall receive me?

6

The final trees seed.
I've caught rides
        in drier deserts.
Where there's salt,
    there's a good sea.

        I've bled through birds, sweated
out acorns, shores.
What happens in heaven stays.
    The final breath says *shh*.
Blueberries carried in an open book.
They fell where I read
lower in bushes
        thankfully not turning a page.

7

Different water to look at in places.
I have lived beside it always,
    no need to mention. Other constants
always implied:
love's everlasting unleadening,
our lightest coats.

    We could stay here, with geese
at the horizon's throat.
Thirty years
isn't old for a well.
        Lift my head, drink what you find.

8

Facts never overlap.
Each continues,
   un-coincident, if we "envision ourselves
in ecology's most intimate appearances,
     but even then there is reason for wonder."

Beloved, the world
   is still around. I've seen it
in a threadbare blouse.
No,
     threadbare is just the hem.
Most nights,
   most nights.
I would end
     with wind showing which.
It does.

9

Facts aren't arguments, as much as
inevitable, by which you should understand
    my hand here lighter.
Having been ruined for forever,
sunrise
      uses all its chalk
on a single stone.

    Between choice and decision,
birds high in the cathedral,
like clover. She put a small plant
    in a cup of stones. The ungraspable
stays close enough.
Falling asleep
      in the most natural light.

10

Anything helps. The obligation
    of the possible. The disproportionate
        love of epigraphs.
Child on the tracks
and the train don't come.
    Like lemons and hairpins
are God's pilot lights.

The dream requires
    extracting the lost child whole
from what we call
catastrophic mud. Breathe
    toward where her mouth must be
but also
continue digging.
        While a hawk turns, nuanced, spare,
in grove dust. Noon is early
and nothing new.

11

Now the theme song starts,
at least a note.
    Fire hydrant
relaxes into reeds.
       The first seeded emerge late
spread by birds
spreading only themselves
      as far as we can see.
Much as the careful interval
of sure rain
in all honesty.

      In all honesty, honesty's not
an even-planted row.
It has a ravaged aspect
akin to an etching notable not
for its execution
    but for being
       the oldest extant replica.

12

Pasture, idyll and gaze.
How could interloper eros not astound
   in its rented carriage, today.
In its regrettable sweater!
     With that familiar, fatalistic emphasis
almost clairvoyant and so
almost already past, an understanding
   one doesn't want, it's something
     past wanting,
and astounds.

Beloved, the ultimatum
never manifests.
There is a further precipice, and time
   isn't anything to be endured.
Maroon
moss. I don't see how anyone could have a child
    except at the shore.

13

    Pelicans in the distance,
flower ships. One river
enough for a city.
    One bridge
for a river.

To tune to something other than the note.
To play the instant steadily behind the beat.
It also keeps.
    Can we return
to June?
Sure.
In eleven months.

14

For now the least wind moves the leash
hanging by the door
        and this hound
heaves.

One could make a list of things that feel
        exactly like reading.
            Standing at a window, watching somebody
open an umbrella.

15

For my part, I can't not prove
the blameless yet hardly faultless last summer
of blue crabs on earth
            doesn't flinch the dogwood close.
My prophecy is only
of the next instant. I will still
be holding this knife
I am holding.
        I can see it. And the pepper veined.

Hands hard down the thighs. The kettle's water
resolving into steam
        years before the whistle. I hold on
to these exceedingly original tomatoes.
Original
because it is winter or
summer and
        I want them or
you brought them. The same tomatoes later aren't.
        Hands down the thighs hard.

16

Other days held on
for days like this, younger
    than any beginning, in certain
singular purples
cast by bronze, by wind's premises,
by forsythia beautiful in another month.
It was a world
    if you walked in it,
long enough to wish to stay, reprieve and later
reprieve, each explanation
another example,
the words for further still including
    further and
        further still.

And warm is always close. They remodel
    the run-down apartment by adding
more garlands each morning.
If I move now as though
always in a photograph you positioned
    an ocean
behind me and near.

17

Or if I listen as you, or endeavor
    to have something to tell so I see
the neighborhood florist doesn't have
        the most beautiful greenhouse.
    It has
the most beautiful greenhouse
    a neighborhood florist has.

Then I have survived for this.
        The standards play themselves
    one note a day.

18

      I clear the trail by running.
Once,
I saw a trillium
so now rightfully expect
    trillium trillium
trillium
ridge.

But why attend to what's already true?
A *help wanted* sign up
    before anyone knows what the business is.
Sunporch next door,
in which my neighbor sings to a child
    simply the bassline—*trillium trillium*
trillium ridge.

19

And birds in the hedge
        are just birds in a hedge.
Wind here
is something else.
It gets in.
    In the tree that never leafs,
yet lives.
Olive tree.

    It happens in no time.
Gold-parched winter grass,
not parched,
holding in
toward another year.

20

Forever has already outdone itself.
Wrens beginning
in straw. The invention of prettiness
beginning in the placement
of a cut blossom in a thumb-vase.
You cut it and keep it
alive with the tenderest.

Snow begins
in a June bay. I come in and immediately
set in
on the dishes.
They don't need to be washed from anything
but being left in the cupboard so long.

21

      Have you come back,
in the hospitable thrall
in which one hangs a wet coat
    by nailing it to the wall?
And the "practical
rabble of grackles," the "undeniable
entirety of sky"— ·
      other phrases
that kept me alive.

Epistle, idyll and far. Soul singing its one
      wanting song—mild
hustle—outside the diner. Pay for this
once. Diners
wave it along. Later
      holding a door at the station,
demanding a tip.
    Later offering a handstand
passing for acrobatic.

22

I burn my tongue
to see if it's warm. It's not enough
but I trust
what isn't. Happiness
happens twice,
like flannel. And snow survives
    between vast appearances
in the lost dog of any honest phrase.

So wit lets go.
Wind-shod,
        the loons cheer.
As the day's only heat
    starts under the coffee
        and the early safety
    of splintered light
comes apart in a prism of cream.
Put any sprig
in this bottle.
It becomes a vase.

23

Reel-to-reel rapture
of sprig dusk, its roadblock, you have to
take the long way
to morning. The painter of sunsets concludes
by painting each roof
reflectively bare.
You can see it: each shadow
    occupies itself exactly,
like salt on a grape.
The horizon vanishes, regarding itself.
No need for Orpheus, in the new translation.
As the inside of a vase
must be prettiest.
It's where the flowers are.
And death isn't closer than any year.

Therefore,
I dreamt I traveled to attend
    the Unsealing of the Poets
from their winter cabin.
        Locals
with axes and stew.
What will they have written?
    I was more eager to see this one's
eyes in the meadow.

24

Beloved, I believe all theories
reduce to the horizontal.
Consider
a gardener hosing hanging plants
        clearing the horizon.
    Or wildflowers
immoderately set.
Ice with no one skating there,
    the familiar
weight of a bow
a violinist's hand
rises without.

    Or a forgotten disquisition
on the fineness of fineness.
    Better to say nothing,
but some things
are better than better.
My toolbox
    heavy with silk tools
and the hurt light.
        They fix enough.

25

Like any children's tale
        the afternoon begins
with a character you cannot tell
from you. So many beliefs
notable today only
for how one cannot retain them
yet can say little else.
Sawdust remains my signal.
Radios rarely on now
except in unfinished homes.
Meadow in every
leveled plot. Riddle: what's
        moving in the trees? The leaves,
and two birds.

Beloved, you don't need to know the language
        to know it's language.
Or once a bird sang in the boughs
        and you swore a flock lives in the boughs.

ACKNOWLEDGMENTS

Many thanks to the editors of the publications in which earlier editions of these poems appeared: the *Bennington Review*, *Big Big Wednesday*, *Broadsided*, *Dusie*, the *Equalizer*, *February*, the *Spectacle*, *Sprung Formal*, *Under a Warm Green Linden*, and the *Volta*.